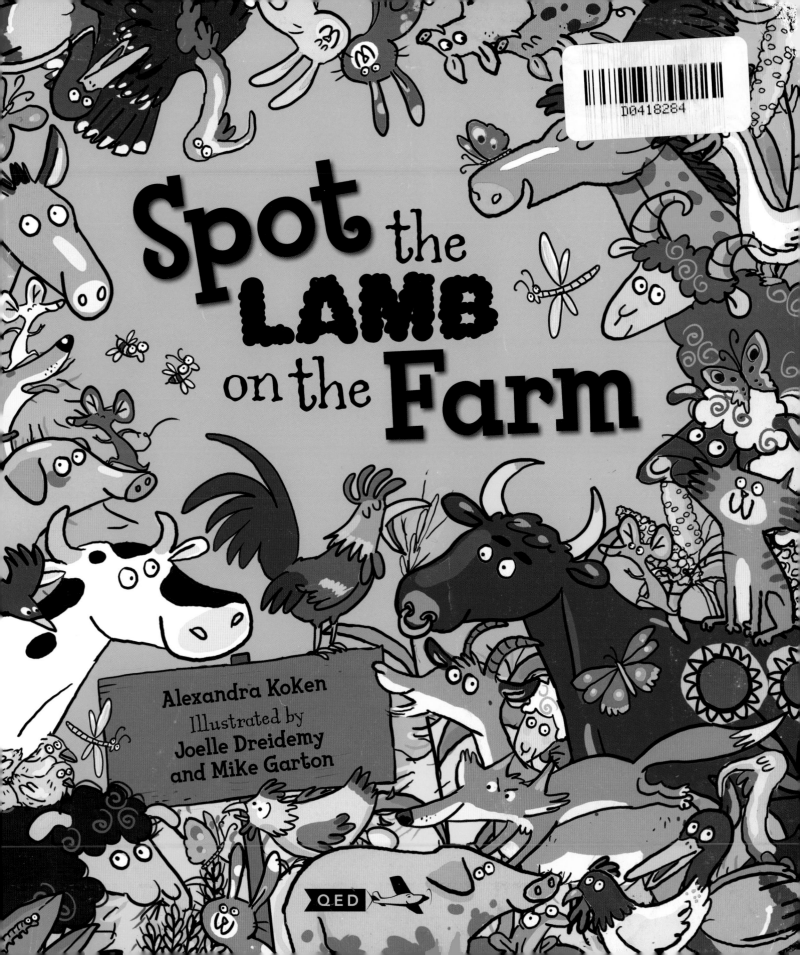

Spot the LAMB on the Farm

Alexandra Koken

Illustrated by
Joelle Dreidemy
and Mike Garton

QED

Sheep

Farm vehicles

Wheat

Cows

Stables

This lamb is hiding inside the book. Can you find her in every scene?

Can you spot these things?

cat   flower   frog   kettle   shoe

Cock-a-doodle-doo!

Donkeys love to make friends with other animals.

Can you spot these things?

umbrella · book · trampoline · green apple · towel

Mud helps pigs to cool down.

Chickens sleep above the ground on a bar called a perch.

Can you spot these things? donkey pants duck spoon bell

Tractors are slow, but very powerful.

When they were first discovered, carrots were purple!

Can you spot these things?

squirrel   worm   button

onion   pumpkin

Can you spot these things?

cow   toothbrush   cupcake   spider's web   chicken

There are hundreds of types, or breeds, of horses.

Bread, pasta and cereals are often made from wheat.

Can you spot these things? watch scales tyre comb sock

A sheep's fleecy coat can be used to make wool.

More to spot

Go back and find these scenes in the book!

Did you find me?

Did you Know?

A chicken can lay about 300 eggs per year. That's almost one a day!

Sheep eat for about seven hours every day.

After cows have swallowed their food, it comes back into their mouths so they can chew it again.

Pigs are very clever and friendly. They make great pets!

A single ant can lift 20 times its body weight. That's like you lifting a tiger!

More farm fun!

Farm sounds

The animals in this book make very different sounds, from "Moo" to "Meow" and "Cock-a-doodle-doo". When you see an animal in the book, make the sound!

Hide and seek

Choose a cuddly toy that you can hide around your home for a friend or family member to spot, just like the lamb in the book! You could hide other objects and make a list of things to find.

Veg patch

Growing vegetables is fun! You can grow small plants such as cress or herbs at home, or bigger plants such as tomatoes and carrots in a garden. You'll need seeds, earth, sunshine and water. Remember to ask an adult for permission and help!

Life cycles

Use books or the Internet to learn about the life cycle of some of the animals you've seen in this book. For example, an egg is laid by an adult chicken, which then hatches into a chick. The chick grows into an adult, and lays more eggs itself.

Q Quarto Knows

Quarto is the authority on a wide range of topics.
Quarto educates, entertains and enriches the lives of our readers—enthusiasts and lovers of hands-on living.
www.quartoknows.com

Designer: Krina Patel
Managing Editor: Victoria Garrard
Design Manager: Anna Lubecka

Copyright © QED Publishing 2016

www.quartoknows.com/brand/2040/QED-Publishing/

First published in hardback in the UK in 2015 by QED Publishing
Part of the Quarto Group, The Old Brewery, 6 Blundell Street, London, N7 9BH

A catalogue record for this book is available from the British Library.

ISBN 978 1 78171 143 9

Printed in China